Guess What

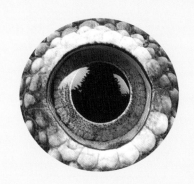

Published in the United States of America by
Cherry Lake Publishing
Ann Arbor, Michigan
www.cherrylakepublishing.com

Content Adviser: Susan Heinrichs Gray
Reading Adviser: Marla Conn, ReadAbility, Inc.
Book Design: Felicia Macheske

Library of Congress Cataloging-in-Publication Data

Calhoun, Kelly, author.
 Twisty tails / Kelly Calhoun.
  pages cm. — (Guess what)
 Summary: "Young children are natural problem solvers and always looking for answers, especially when it involves animals. Guess
What: Twisty Tails provides young curious readers with striking visual clues and simply written hints. Using the photos and text,
readers rely on visual literacy skills, reading, and reasoning as they solve the animal mystery. Clearly written facts give readers a
deeper understanding of how the animal lives. Additional text features, including a glossary and an index, help students locate
information and learn new words."— Provided by publisher.
 Audience: Ages 5-8
 Audience: K to grade 3
 Includes index.
 ISBN 978-1-63362-628-7 (hardcover) — ISBN 978-1-63362-718-5 (pbk.) — ISBN 978-1-63362-808-3 (pdf) —
ISBN 978-1-63362-898-4 (ebook)
 1. Chameleons—Juvenile literature. 2. Children's questions and answers. I. Title.

QL666.L23C35 2016
597.95'6—dc23

2015003102

Cherry Lake Publishing would like to acknowledge the work of The Partnership for 21st Century Skills.
Please visit *www.p21.org* for more information.

Printed in the United States of America
Corporate Graphics Inc.

Table of Contents

I have eyes that see well up close.

And my eyes can move in many directions.

I have **feet** that can **grasp** branches.

My tail can coil around things.

I like to
hang around
in trees.

13

My rough skin can change colors.

I have a very long tongue.

17

Yum!

I like to eat insects.

Do you know what I am?

I'm a Chameleon!

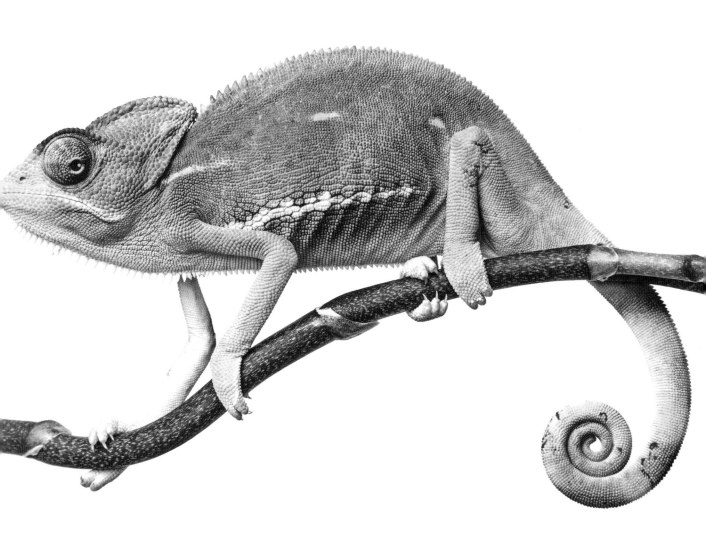

About Chameleons

1. Chameleons have very long tongues.

2. Chameleons can purposely change the color of their skin. This is how they talk to one another.

3. Chameleons' eyeballs can move separately.

4. The biggest chameleons are as large as cats.

5. Young chameleons are able to hunt right after after they **hatch**.

Glossary

coil (coyl) to wind into loops or rings

directions (duh-REK-shunz) the lines along which something moves or points

grasp (grasp) to grab something and hold it tightly

hatch (hach) to break out of an egg

insects (IN-sektz) a small animal with six legs and three main body parts

Index